ASTERISMS

T0273583

ASTERISMS

✷ poems ✷

donna kane

HARBOUR PUBLISHING

Harbour Publishing Co. Ltd.
P.O. Box 219, Madeira Park, BC, VON 2H0
www.harbourpublishing.com

Edited by Peter Midgley
Cover design by Libris Simas Ferraz
Text design by Carleton Wilson
Printed and bound in Canada
Printed on 100% recycled paper

Harbour Publishing acknowledges the support of the Canada Council for the Arts, the Government of Canada, and the Province of British Columbia through the BC Arts Council.

LIBRARY AND ARCHIVES CANADA CATALOGUING IN PUBLICATION

Title: Asterisms : poems / Donna Kane.
Names: Kane, Donna (Poet), author.
Identifiers: Canadiana (print) 20230568475 | Canadiana (ebook) 20230568483 | ISBN 9781990776717 (softcover) | ISBN 9781990776724 (EPUB)
Subjects: LCGFT: Poetry.
Classification: LCC PS8621.A54 A92 2024 | DDC C811/.6—dc23

for Wayne

On Visible Light

Knowledge is the fruiting body of light,
and light the fruiting body of photons
at the end of travelling through our nights
to reach the velvet chair, the common snipe,
where we see that in an object's reflection,
knowledge is the fruiting body of light.
Just a slice of electromagnetic
wavelength and sight is ours, a blindness gone
at the end of travelling through our nights.
All this way and yet something's not right.
This blue colour we see is the chair's rejection.
Knowledge is the fruiting body of light
whose shadow dogs us. Might this be the heart
of why we fail to reach satisfaction
at the end of travelling through our nights.
Always wanting what is beyond our sight,
always drawn toward the parts still hidden.
Knowledge is the fruiting body of light
at the end of travelling through our nights.

Table of Contents

✳ ✳ ✳

✳ ✳ ✳

✳ ✳ ✳

✳ ✳ ✳

*** *** ***

Wayfinder

I just want to be happy.
I like the springtime sounds of wood frogs.
I think an earthworm's five hearts are sweet.
I don't like to think of the world as bloodied.
I wish you'd never told me that dropping
a spider from an upstairs window
is not always an act of hospitality.
Yes, bumblebees are desiccating,
pine siskins are collapsing in our festering trays,
but have you any idea how tired I feel?
The last time I looked inside a darkened room,
it hit me. All this worrying about what will become
of Earth's vibrancy or imagination's capacity
is moot: we won't know our imagination's
shrivelled because we'll have nothing left
to compare ourselves to. And if there's nothing
beyond our self-preoccupation, no tender recall
of speckled trout or gulls gliding above the smokestacks,
or a trail dappled by a thousand flickering willow leaves,
then where's the worry, what's to miss?

Is That a Spit of Rain I Hear or Shrapnel from an Asteroid?

Oh Dimorphos, little moonlet born into our imagination
by your wavering light now destined to be a skewered
kebab or at the very least nicked to change the speed
of your orbit around Didymos, the potentially hazardous
near-Earth object of the Apollo group you cling to.
It's never easy when two objects want to be in the same
place at the same time. At the intended kerthump,
imagine Edgerton's *Milk Drop Coronet* to the prelude
of *Also sprach Zarathustra* while we take God into
our own hands. In truth, I've had more near misses
than collisions, more coming so close to being struck
by pickup trucks gunning lefts through traffic-controlled
crosswalks than I care to recall, precursors as they are
to the souped-up grill that will do us both in, ejecting
plumes of what bound us, a glowing debris
returned to little more than ash.

Starry Night, *Vincent van Gogh*

My father, more pragmatic than unkind, observed
I was, at the age of five, unfit for survival
were it not for the invention of corrective lenses.

My first pair of glasses was blue, flecked with silver.
I thought they were beautiful—words on the page!
leaves on the trees! the stars!—when I read van Gogh

may have been a myope too, painting as he did half-blind,
I removed my glasses, and peered at the frizzed-out sky
and thought of how the Alpilles appeared so often

in van Gogh's work, the hills dividing the earth
from the constellations. I'd imagine myself a roiling speck.
In one version, circled by vultures, in another, lighting the sky.

Comet NEOWISE, 2020

A briefly struck match igniting the leading
question—how did we get to be where we are?
Sublimation powders the chambers of our
empty ice cube trays, bursts of curiosity

subside to *"The nights were cloudy." "I forgot to look
up."* Comas of self-absorption envelop our
imperfect orbits. What we should have asked—
how do we learn to be where we are—grows

fuzzy, more nebulous with each pass.

James Webb Telescope at the Lagrange Point 2 (L2)

Dear beryllium gold-plated mirror the size of a tennis court
parked at the second of two balance points, does gravity
cancelled out feel like the liminal space between each moment
that might just be the massless glue of thought? Do you feel a bit
like consciousness, that you're being held within bodies,
gathering information before you drift away? When forces
come to zero, do you feel you're in a place that no longer exists?
Should I think of where you are as death? As all our deaths?
We can predict where it will be. We can measure its zero force.
But once we arrive, there's nothing there.

The Big Bounce

Some say it's not the universe
that's so interesting, but what turns
it on and off. Like you and me,
baby—how we met, what brought
us to the brink. If every start
follows a previous close and every
ending precedes a new beginning,
then maybe we are a version
of the cosmos—when we're getting
it on, we're the centre, our spiral galaxies
and nebulae huffing inside our skins
and when we call it quits, we're just
bouncing through another phase.
There's a lot to be said for this theory,
not the least of which is love.

Perennial

All day, birdsong tills the air.
By evening, stars push through

the loam, perennial, their roots
tapping back to the bulb of their first

blossoming. It's not the flight so much
as how the sparrow gathers up her body

for the landing, how the ladybug folds
each wing like a napkin inside its lacquered

case. How we are designed to open as much
as we are to close. Listen to the frog's singing.

How it starts as suddenly as it stops.

Raindrop Creates a Rainbow After Meeting a Shaft of Light

I was a raindrop, transparent,
but denser than what you were
used to. When your light entered me,
I got so excited, I fell into
the groove of you, reflecting
your dispersions into bands
of yes, yes, yes while all around me,
a massacre of other possibilities.
A reflection of a refraction
refracting, what I emitted was
all me. What was seen was all you.

Artemis Program, or My Last Moon Poem

Hey, big round of cheese, ejectum
from some ancient collision, listen up.
We're headed your way, and this time
we're bringing pyjamas. If you're sick
and tired of moon poems, this is your
lucky day. Once we've staked our
claim on you, you'll be no different
to those still here on Earth than looking
across a prairie so open we can see
all the way to Alberta. We'll look up
and mostly wonder who's on you,
who's brushing their teeth, setting their clocks,
bickering over unwashed cups. You'll cease
to be our expansive gaze, imagination's room
of its own. I know we've weeded out wonder
before, but this one takes the cake.
Or should I say pizza pie.

Weather Station in the Alpine above Nonda Creek

Both the whirligig and the buttercup
point in the gust's direction. The depth
of moss and the compass indicate north.
The slant of squat stems and the blur

in a weathervane's blades register velocity
of wind. At some point we wanted to get
ahead of ourselves. If we couldn't control
the weather, at least we would know

what was coming. It was the beginning of day
after day, contraption after contraption, a jittery
sense of being lost to the world, to gadgets
tethered to patches of lichen-scraped ground,

to numbers repeating inside our heads.

Nonda Creek Alpine

When the buzz of a hoverfly turns to a whine
that's a mind homing in on their subject:
the salt on my canvas shoe or a way out
of the tent, an orange gill pegged

to the top of Mount Nonda, inhaling
the alpine winds, exhaling crackles
and flaps. In every direction more mountains
where sockets of snow out-stare patches

of buttercups, the wool of the about-to-bloom
lousewort. But if I stand in the snow,
it's the flowers that beckon, my senses
drawn to wherever I'm not.

Surely, breath's rhythm is the heart of want—
in and then out, in and then out.

Luminosities

Startled, the snow buntings rise
from the cropped field, hundreds
of flickering stars, the space between
our bodies enough to avoid
collision but so close I can
feel their wing-thrummed air,
the elastic tether of their movement,
each bird a composite of the single

swerve. Tingling with the fade
of their nickering wings, the birds
settle back into the stubble.
Crouched, they still sing, the ground
symphonic with buzz and warble.
The hawk coasting with determined calm.

The Present

The unfurling leaf slips off
its celery glove, and the wind
blasts the shell dry before
it hits the ground. The present
never stood a chance, a pale
sheath sailing between verge
and gone, birth and death,
twin shores impossible to grasp.

Spring

Oh, habitable zone, home closer. Let
me feel your effervescent leaves unfurl.

Let me hear, pond to pond, each dialect
of frog, each bubble-gum bellow birth.
Oh, carbonaceous flowering, let your lilac
blossoms cloak a bird on every limb. Earth

has given us its winter to work our grudges
through. From under rot and bitter husks,
the perennial crocus blooms. With every
opened flower, it thinks itself anew.

Pigs

I was surprised to learn pigs have the capacity to dream,
their own language, can recognize their name at two weeks,
sing to their babies. I'm not surprised, by now, that we can slice
their head in two, their temporal bone excellent for training
in human ear surgery. That their valves work in the human heart
remains surprising. Did you know a pig will eat a human,
leaving only their dentures behind? Did you know that humans
will eat pigs, leaving only their ears—though sometimes those too
if they use a kitchen torch to remove the hairs, then scrub
them like the ears of children: boil, slice, fry. Some scientists
say the similarity between humans and pigs is mostly happenstance,
not a sign of close ancestry. Not as if we are family.

Cleaning Up before We Go

It's like wearing clean underwear
should the paramedics fail to revive us.
The dish cloth folded overtop the spout
of the kitchen faucet, the puckered cushion
propped, just so, on our favourite chair.
Don't we all want to present our best selves
when we leave? So everyone will know we cared?
But look at us. Jesus. The unprecedented wind's
knocked over a trash can and there's shit
up and down the street—wet wipes and granola bar
wrappers, plastic straws and Timmie cups.
The streetlights are throwing moths off course,
and no one's sleeping. They're putting toe tags
on birds whacking our high rises. We're like toddlers—
four and a half billion years, and you can't leave us
alone for six million.

On Silence

If one thing must relate to another
for meaning to cohere, you don't want
to be alone in the world. Except I do.
Especially on summer nights when
I lie on my back, look up at the sky
and listen to the dark until I feel myself
as silence, the silence between a caragana
pod snapping and a dried begonia blossom
falling to the deck, between the swirls
of sparrow song and each star as it appears.
It is then I feel I can know the world,
the way music can be disclosed only
by the silence between each note.
And the silence before. And after.

On Avoidance

Once I hoped frost would kill all
the nasturtiums. I was tired of watering
them, but didn't want their death
pinned on me. This might not seem
as bad as if I hoped the man who trails me
down the street for cash, which I give
him, would overdose so I could walk
without harassment to the home
décor store to buy stainless steel
bar tongs. But it is. It is. "I've made it
through another year," I'll say, though
much of it was focused elsewhere,
and what I mean is, I'm one year closer
to the end without being the moral
degenerate I suspect I really am.
Afraid of what's inside, I distract myself
from myself, watch sunset after sunset.
The never here, the never now.

On Uncertainty

When the buzzer sounds and the school doors
open, and our children tumble out like suitcases
onto the carousel, of course I'll know which one
is mine. It's a mild panic, but if I don't spot
my Samsonite, then surely its red luggage tag.
If not my child, her pompom toque.
Do I really believe we won't recognize each other,
that the ties of love criss-crossing so assuredly
at drop-off would disentangle by three?
Do I believe our planet won't flick
us away with a twitch of its skin at any given
moment? That the familiar face of the sun
each morning is the same as knowing
we'll wake up again?

On Memory

The bee converts honey into wax the way senses
produce slivers of thought shaped into cells
that hold what we remember, capped until
there is nothing to nourish us but that summer
afternoon when we drank wine on the deck
and wasps landed on the rims of our glasses,
and a friend let them meander around her hand
and up her arm, the wasps stopping now
and then to wash their whiskers. Miles Davis
was playing. In this memory, there was time and space
for everyone. This memory, which is no longer
that afternoon, but nectar in an uncapped cell,
a sweetness between before and after.

On Finding a Dead Pigeon on Argyle Street

Morning, and Earth's spinning-raffle-drum has chosen us again.
Outside my bedroom window, I hear your low, sweet cries

rounding up your iridescent kin. Pestering the cat. Oh, lapsed
herbivore, our blackened branch diverging me from you

still burns, my anthropomorphic ways deemed self-obsessed,
to which I cry foul. And you. They call you *gutter bird*, leave you

on the street to die. When headlines say your mate looked like
she was going to cry, the claim's decried. It's not *real* mourning.

It's just an instinctive gesture to survive while you identify our tumours,
understand space and time, learn our alphabet, find your way home blind.

Familiarity Breeds Contempt; or, I Woke Up and Couldn't Breathe

First the alarm, phones sounding
a sonic dread, then orders to evacuate.
Forewarned then fired, the word now
drifting ash on our hair and bed.

I always thought contempt was a form
of hatred, but it's more than that.
It's when we feel a subject's beneath
consideration. Deserving, even,

of our scorn. We insisted on what
nature might provide. Whether smoke
or nimbus, the blackened sky didn't
seem so bad. It's never seemed so bad.

We sleep, open-mouthed, lungs filling,
filling, with the particulates of our disdain.

Perched as I Feel, between Inner and Outer

In the produce section, surrounded by the outer glow
of lemons and nectarines, the pebbled topographies

of avocadoes, I'm struck by the world's impermeability—
I'll never see my face in three dimensions. I'll never see my four-chambered

heart. Not to mention Earth's inner core. The waxed skins of fruit
shine as if the surface of things were mostly bling, but deep

inside the stomach's pit we wait for the rind to be peeled, the systems
within to fall apart. In the aisle of squash varietals, I shift my weight

as though testing the planet's crust, then the meat of the mantle below.
And underneath that, in its own solitude, the molten outer core

which at this very moment thrums with a magnetic field shielding
me and the blueberries in their breathable baskets from

killer radiation hurled by our life-giving star. I know
I should let it go and just enjoy the collisions—nozzles misting

the rutabagas, spray landing on my membrane of skin.
My mouth breathing in, and then, as all ruined things re-seed,

breathing out, chanting to myself—*the purpose of the sun is to be*
the sun, the Earth to be the Earth, the peach the peach. I should focus

on things I can control, but what might that be? I can't
even open the plastic bag to slip my Honey Crisp apples inside.

Excursions

I am walking on a trail that runs north–south,
following the hoof prints of a moose whose
cloven steps press bar magnets into the earth.
Above me, red winged blackbirds swoop

from talcumed aspen to blooming saskatoon,
wind-loosened petals scattering
the path like metal filings pointed in
the gust's direction. *Do you think you're lost?*

jeers reason. I think of the feet of swallowtails
tasting the rue before laying their eggs
on the blades of grass. Of the spider who plucks
the web of a mate to let them know

they're not prey. How once we too served sense
and reason as equal points on a compass.

Peace

The magpie and the cat
sit together on the deck,
a few inches apart, each
the other's threshold.
Were the magpie any smaller,
the cat would kill the bird.
Were the magpie any bigger,
the bird would kill the cat.
I wish this wasn't how
peace worked, but there
they are, side by side,
pretending they don't see each other.
I'll take it. Bless it even.

When June Turns to July

June is a spool racer, winding up its rubber band
of stored energy, and July is letting it unfurl.
Fruit kicking off its blooms, lime darkening
to green, eggshells crumbling in the grass.
Frogs that ratcheted past solstice now mated and silent.
Caught in the backwards spin, we feel ourselves in free fall,
unwhirling through sepaled, berried, shrinking light.

The Observable Universe

In my greenhouse, one tiny grain
containing every speck of energy

propels itself outward into stalks and leaves
and blossoms and too many cucumbers to count.
The centre now everywhere.

When did looking back solve anything,
when did knowing where we came
from change where we are? Still,

we crave root's tang on our tongue,
its pungent liquid, mineral and gas,
whiff of bitter and of sweet.

Swallowtail Butterfly

Little asteroid sucked through the open door,
drawn to the window's walled light where you
batted the glass, your yellow and black scales breaking
off, falling to the sill, the magnified sun burning
your thinning wings. Cupped in my hands
like a sliver of meteorite, I was startled
by your weight. When I carried you outside, opened
the orb of my fingers, you wheeled away as though
you'd nicked a gravity well and were bouncing
from the graze—a flare of scattering light.

August Dusk

Tonight, the wind is on muscle relaxants,
a kindled loose-lipped billowing that sifts through
my cells and the brittle stems of Roundup-Ready
canola. On the smoke-caramelized horizon,
the International Space Station sails its seed of light
with the intent and purpose of something
without intent or purpose. Kin to
wreckage, beauty persists. The wind,
doctored with formaldehyde and
benzene, lulls us to sleep. All night,
we are hungry for its warmth.

Grotesques

With a flyswatter, my Facebook friend has snapped
a wasp in two—falling to the placemat, its body waves
a jointed leg; on its patch-quilt head, antennae
lift like solar sensors. We say we're torn, but watch

as each new posting charts the hours for the head to die
and hours more while the body remains alive, making its way
across the fabric the way someone shot through the chest
might pull themselves toward the phone. I really must go

outside. Above me, stars are bobbing to the surface, each with
its own diagnosis until the sky's so full it's all in the same condition.
They say every living thing sheds photons. If our eyes were
differently tweaked, we'd see the light that emits from us all.

August Is a Dance Hall at 3 a.m.

Pollen stuck to its feet like grains of floor wax,
the bee's dancing slows but doesn't stop.
It waits for last call, for frost's biting light
to snap back on. Among the flower's popped
balloons, it knows it's time, but it can't go home.
Spiked with Earth's tilt, the bee must play
it out—the dance, the drink, the drained cup.

Still Life of Pears on the Macdonald Bridge

Whether art or impulse, the can of *No Name* pears
on the pedway railing of the Macdonald Bridge,
its yellow label flashing 52,000 vehicles a day,
could be likened to an underwing moth. The steel
deck, grey clouds, cold sea, is the insect's closed
wings. When the travellers catch sight of the can's
bright colour, that's the hindwings opening as the moth
takes flight. Or maybe the can, rising out of the fog,
could be seen as the pivotal moment when the first star
formed, the water-packed Bartletts, deep within their cosmic
dawn, fusing the grit and sweet of our shared elements,
the salt air oxidizing the lid on our precarious futures.
For those who would describe the event as a can of halved
pears that stayed in place for several weeks before someone
carted it off, don't you miss it a little, as landmark,
as waypoint, as that much closer to arriving back home?

September, Thinking of the Worker Wasp I Crashed
Into This Summer

Intent on crumpling flecks of weathered deck
inside your mouth, you launched from your planet
of ribboned pulp, just as I, interstellar object
on a mission to a glass of wine, crossed your flight

path—wallop to you, sting to me, your venom
exciting my pain receptors, my cheek
swelling like your nest, which kept growing
from the inside out. I thought of doing you in,

but season's end comes soon enough. Amphoras
of spit emptying out their hearts.
Is that you dragging your starving husk across
the floor? Here, drink this sugared water.

Each of us takes that final breath.
Exhales—we hope, sated.

To an Observer

They say objects appear to take up more
space when they move, but I am not so sure.
The arms of the chair implore me to sit,
but its emptiness has a grim reaper's air.

And the robins. Today they flocked up,
the yard a frenzy of bodies grown plump
with berries and fruit. In fevered flight, one
thumped the window, and the bird fell

stunned to the ground. The chair
you no longer sit in, the feather
greased to the pane, fills the space
as expectantly as voices and flight.

What's stilled waits to be moved.
What moves waits to be stilled.

Luck

For a time, I imagined only awful scenarios.
This was not because I was preparing
for the worst, but because nothing ever
went as planned. My strategy, then,

to imagine every awful thing to ensure
it never happened. If I did voice wishful
thoughts, I'd rap my pine desk so the wood's
good spirits would wake and pay attention. Some say

you can find luck anywhere; others say you can't.
Then the awful thing happened even though I'd
envisioned it. Then someone said they'd thought
the awful thing and that is why it happened.

Then I was told it was evil spirits, not well wishers,
in the wood of my desk and knocking was not
so they'd hear, but so they wouldn't. I saw my
gestures didn't count. I saw only the great unknown.

Beauty

Dreading the end of beauty, I harvested
pods before they were full, cut blossoms
before gravity hunted them down, obscured
the truth the way snow blankets what's soon
to be worm food, saying *passed, gone to spirit,*
instead of *dead.* But the pink light of morning
could not be stopped, nor the flower's first bloom
or the bright stain of strawberries which I did not resist.
I saw that beauty cannot be stayed.
To be here at all is to swim its current through.

Life as Silk Rug

There are days the past gathers around me like the flowered rug
I once passed out on, my friends rolling me up inside it—
an extravagant plushness and the fret of suffocation.

Other days it feels like having dropped thousands of worms
into vats of boiling water for a gram of silk—
more has been lost than gained.

In the earth's warp and weft, my remaining threads
to be knotted are countable. Today, everywhere
I walk is woven with the past.

This shape will hold, I tell myself, this tapestry of which we're
each a part. Like the carpet of stars that seems never to change
though always, some are winking in, some are winking out.

Jet Lag

Age is a place we learn about from brochures
or hearsay. We think we know its nights,
its days, its pros and cons, its notable sights
as though we've been there, but they're feathers

stuck to the pavement. They're not the bird.
And though everyone's future lies fallow
before them, we still say, *I don't feel my age,*
as if we knew what that was before arrival.

Face it, we're dizzy with the heights, wondering
if we should hit the bar or dress up formal, struggling
to align our internal clock with the local time,
hoping we've packed for the weather.

Blown Glass

When senses fizzle and thought gutters out,
memories, like blown glass, crack, pop, melt
back into the ether. If we think of our lives
as brief, we forget a salmon's migration,
a butterfly's wing whose scales remember
the stare of an owl. We forget the single
lung of earth—how it holds the atoms
of all that's been breathed, and will be.
Even now, air, hot from my body,
draws deep into the wood of the willow
to one day release into the life of a bee.

Can You Give Me My Little Skull?

My senses are trick-or-treaters, gathering stimuli
that my brain, like any good mother,
checks out first, deciding what I can have—
yes to the man with the wiener dog walking past
my house, no to the pigeons leaving tracks in the snow,
to bells ringing the hour at the memorial tower.
Such a theory suggests I am missing a lot.
I suppose I am, though I suspect I'm partly to blame.
I believe in carrying the burdens of the world, but sometimes
I need to lie down and close my eyes for just a moment.
Tonight, the brain gave me an idea sweet as a Molasses Kiss,
but when I reached my journal, the thought was gone.
I know I was given something before it disappeared,
but you can't ask the brain, she's head down,
rummaging through the chaos, unwrapping
then tossing me each approved thing
like she never needs to see it again.

The Incredible Hulk

Like that marvel of science
Bruce Banner, who watches his body
expand, buttons popping
from his shirt, disclosing the Hulk,
so I watch my body fall apart,
disclosing time. Both Bruce and I
unwitting and without a cure.
But does the Hulk, once disclosed,
also disclose Bruce Banner?
Does time, once disclosed,
also disclose me? They say music
discloses the fabric of the universe,
but is not the universe,
so there's that, I say to my friend.
The two of us are discussing old
television shows and time's passage,
drinking cider from apples
that fell to the ground, disclosing
gravity. Though it's not so much
the apples that fell, my friend says,
as it was the tree that dropped them.
All those delicate white blossoms
transforming into fruit, swelling
until the green apples became
too heavy to hold. We agree
something else is afoot,
but neither of us can grasp it.

Morning Thoughts of Death While Watching a Horse Cross a Snowy Field

Hooves stethoscope the snow—are we well?
Thickets of kicked-up light, crystals that fall
even as they rise. Coffee cooling as it pours.

Heyday

When I slipped on the ice, my feet
skidding off the deck, yellow toque flying,
I thought, why is it when we give in
to gravity we no longer feel its presence,
only when we're unable to resist its pull
do we feel weightless? I spent the first
part of my life waiting for my heyday,
the last part looking back. I think I was
popular at the time, but I was falling,
too far from the landing to know
I was picking up speed.

Dear Horseshoe Crab,

You must have thought you'd seen it all,
multiple ice ages, Gondwanaland, Pangaea,
dinosaurs, that big asteroid, the Paleozoic,
the Cenozoic. Thank goodness for the moon.
I'll bet the full and the new in May and June
never get old for you. By the way,
how are your four thousand children?

Remember the day my soft mammalian body
scooped you up and brought you into human
taxonomy? I'm sorry our system misnamed you—
not a crab, not even crustaceous. Sometimes
we can be such airheads. And horseshoe?
That word must feel millions of years
after the fact of you, but what I wish to say is

we didn't intend to kill you,
we only wanted your miraculous blood (so blue!)
to clot our endotoxins. And while we
think of you more as safety officer
than aristocrat, monitoring our vaccines,
our chemo infusions, our knee
replacement hardware, you remain
our final word on pure.

I realize when we line up your kin like infantry,
strap their army-helmet carapaces to a metal trench
for sterilization, stick the needle in and drain a third
of their blood, it can't be all that pleasant.
It's also true not all of you survive. I hope you know
we always mean to put you back, but labs are busy places,
which I'm sure your ten eyes can attest to.

This might cheer you—you made the list of *One Hundred Most Important Contributions to Public Health.*
Imagine how many lives you've saved, imagine,
each year, bleeding half a million of you!

And while we're working on a synthetic you,
for now, we must stick to the tried and true.
Maybe when our crises are over, our threats not so dire,
though other concerns will remain for you—
our sea walls, our polluted oceans,
our barbecued street food.

I wish we'd realized sooner how you can't
breed in captivity without a major redo,
that you lay your eggs only in the sand that conceived
you, that you ride in on a springtime tide
when the moon is full or new.

Winter Solstice

In spring I was a compressed bat of bright insulation sliced open,
expanding into every corner until there were no corners.
No one could get a word in edgewise. Where was my head?

Awash in myself, is where. It was like owning the world
without knowing the world at all. But wasn't I beautiful?
Wasn't I outrageous? Was it me or the earth who, after

the long summer, turned away, the sunflower and the poppy
drawing back in. In those waning hours, no one was more surprised
than I was. How I sharpened, became capable of fierce angles

of perspective stretching far across the snow. I began to notice details,
and their undersides, a piece of gravel, a nick in a kitchen drawer.
My shadow grew so long I could see where I was going before I arrived.

Things I Need to Remember if My City Is Invaded

That a single teaspoon of soil holds a billion bacteria,
yards of fungal filaments, thousands of protozoa,
scores of nematodes. That I want there to be room
for everyone. That astronomers look for light's
imperceptible wobble to tell us we're not alone.
That there are more microbial species on Earth
than stars in our galaxy. That I can't give up hope
we'll learn to get along, some quiver of understanding
that there is nothing about us that isn't also something else—
centipede dust, earthworm dust. That we're a funfair house
of mirrors reflecting each other and astronomers
should be careful what they wish for.

New Year's Party

Part Darth Vader, part bathroom fan,
the eight-foot, blow-up snowman is hissing
from his corner of the yard like he's the neighbourhood bully—
"Give me your change. Or else." By morning,
Frosty's a spent condom, a shed skin on the lawn
where starlings grapple with a Hickory Stick,
each of them trying to work it into their beak
before the roughest pigeon, a switchblade tucked
inside a pocket, struts toward the birds who now tremble
the leaves of the swollen rhododendron,
buds prepped for spring, tethering for now the last
Christmas ornaments. I resolve to be positive. I really do.

System of Units or the Grand K or Planck's Constant or $6.62607015 \times 10^{-34}$

Locked deep in a vault in a suburb
of Paris, requiring three keys (only two
kept in France), vacuum-sealed beneath
three glass bells, a cylinder of metal
once embodied a kilogram.

In a living room in Rolla, accessed
through two front doors—one of which
I can't find the key for, the other inside
a canvas shoe, sitting on a worn-out couch,
a lump of flesh and bone embodies me.

The old argument returns—does math
imbue the universe or did we discover
ways to measure it using a capacity for math?
Does the vinegary cinnamon of a pine needle
exist in the tree or does it smell that way through my nose?

When the definition of a kilogram changed
to a mathematical constant determining mass
without reference, that forged chunk
of platinum-iridium whose weight could be felt
in the palm of our hand became the last of its kind.

Last night, the northern lights sieved the stars
like a whale's baleen sieves seawater for krill.
A brisk wind flowed over and around me,
raising the hairs on my arm. I combed
the darkness for what I might find.

Love Poem for Every Animal on Earth

Gravity is a tailor
stitching planets around stars,
pearl buttons cinched tight,

cinched tight in space
like hearts inside the rib cage
of the elephant or the shrew.

The elephant or the shrew,
the me or the you; the number
of heartbeats the same for us all.

The same for us all though some take them fast,
some take them slow. What a beautiful rhythm,
can you feel us? Held together in this world.

Together in this world.

Notes

In "Things I Need to Remember if My City Is Invaded," the lines "a billion bacteria, / yards of fungal filaments, thousands of protozoa, / scores of nematodes" were taken from the web page, "The secret life of garden soil" in *Farm and Dairy*. https://www.farmanddairy.com/news/the-secret-life-of-garden-soil

In "The Present," the lines "sailing between verge / and gone, birth and death, / twin shores impossible to grasp," were inspired by the lines "The time of our lives passes between two black boxes, two Xs, two vanishing poles: unrepresentable, unreachable" from *Philosophy for Passengers* by Michael Marder (MIT, 2022).

In "On Silence," the lines "music can be disclosed only / by the silence between each note" were inspired by ideas in *Alien Listening: Voyager's Golden Record and Music from Earth* by Daniel K.L. Chua and Alexander Rehding (Zone Books, 2021).

Acknowledgements

Sincere thanks to Katherin Edwards for her friendship and writing support, to Lorri Nielsen Glenn for her friendship and generous input into many of the poems in this book, to George Murray and all the participants of his "Walk the Line" workshops and forums. I will always be grateful for that January night in 2021 when I first signed in via Zoom to one of George's workshops. It was exactly what I needed. Many of the poems in this book began in those spaces.

To all the folks at Harbour—thank you for your continuing support of my work and for your belief in the value of books. Sincere appreciation to editor Peter Midgley for his knowledge and exacting eye, and to proofreader Artie Goshulak who not only improved the accuracy of the text but many of the poems as well.

Some of these poems previously appeared in *Arc Poetry* (Arc Award of Awesomeness), *Scientific American* (special thanks to editor Dava Sobel for all of her generosities), the *Temz Review* and *Thimbleberry*. My thanks to all the editors of these publications.

Thank you to the Canada Council for the Arts for providing a grant that allowed me time to write.

And finally, thank you to my family, my sisters for their Sunday emails, Emilie, and to Wayne Sawchuk, my walking resource library on too many subjects to mention and my travelling companion on life's path.